Hope Through the Fire
Winning with the Word and Prayer

Racquel L. Mitchell

©2021 Racquel L. Mitchell. All rights reserved.

No part of this publication may be reproduced, stored in a retrieval system, or transmitted in any form or by any means, electronic, mechanical, photocopying or otherwise, without the written permission of the copyright owner, except for brief quotations used in connection with reviews in magazines or newspapers.

Unless otherwise noted, all Scripture quotations are taken from the Holy Bible, King James Version, which is held in public domain.

Scripture quotations marked (NIV) are taken from the Holy Bible, New International Version ®, NIV ®. Copyright © 1973, 1978, 1984, 2011 by Biblica, Inc.™ Used by permission of Zondervan. All rights reserved worldwide. The "NIV" and "New International Version" are trademarks registered in the United States Patent and Trademark Office by Biblica, Inc.™

To Jesus ---
Thank You for being the Fourth Man in all of my fires.

To my family ---
Thank you for your sacrifices. Your love is a constant source of support.

Table of Contents

Preface 8

<u>Crises with Health</u>
1. **Not Without a Fight** 11
   One man refuses to accept a negative report.

2. **Against the Odds** 13
   A woman with an incurable illness takes matters into her own hands.

3. **Beyond Excuses** 15
   An infirmed man is healed despite his utter despair.

<u>Crises with Personal Struggles</u>
1. **Lord, Fix My Heart**..18
   God uses an uncanny worshipper to revive His people's lukewarm relationship with Him.

2. **Thirsty No More** 20
   A woman wins her battle with addiction.

<u>Crises in Families</u>
1. **A Love That Saves** 23
   A beloved patriarch petitions God for the salvation of his nephew.

2. **Bad Blood** 25
   Unresolved conflict ends favorably despite a deep divide.

3. **Mama Wounds** 27
   A mother influences her daughter to commit socially deviant behavior.

4. **Lord, Have Mercy** 29
   A young woman is raped by her brother.

Crises in Romance
1. **Entangled** 32
   Uncontrollable lust leads to a scandalous and fatal affair.

2. **Save Me** 34
   A troubled marriage is restored.

Crises with Loss
1. **Down But Not Out** 37
   Prayer after unprecedented loss leads to great recovery.

2. **Life After Death** 39
   God restores meaning to a life rocked by grief.

3. **Redeemed** 41
   A woman who loses everything has another chance at her dreams.

Crises with The Church
1. **Down to My Last Dime** 44
   A member's sacrifice is finally acknowledged.

2. **Drowning in Shame** 47
   Christ stands up for a woman experiencing church hurt.

3. **Even Me** 49
   A pastor faces his congregation despite a known affliction.

4. **Yes, Lord** 52
   A minister risks his life to reach the most notorious of sinners.

Crises at Work
1. **Worth the Risk** 55
   Employees risk their jobs to stand up for what is right.

2. **Hater Elevation** 57
   A man rises above his haters' plot to sabotage his career.

Crises in the Country
1. **God First** 60
   God raises up a leader to free His people from oppression.

2. **Heal Our Land** 62
   A man is chosen to lead his native land to salvation.

Preface

Hello, and thank you for reading this book. As I pen this preface, it is March 2021 and the world is a year into the most major, ongoing fire of our time: COVID-19 or the coronavirus pandemic. To date the virus has killed over 2.6 million people worldwide, over 530,000 of whom were of my native country, the United States of America. For months, schools, churches, businesses, and restaurants were shut down, and the world was made to shelter in place. We've had to socially distance and wear masks at almost every public place. Furthermore, many people have lost their jobs, leaving families vulnerable to poverty and homelessness. Last August alone nearly 60 million U.S. citizens filed for unemployment, and at least 4 million of those jobs aren't expected to return. To add to the devastation, racial injustice and police brutality reached a fevered pitch, and mass protests overtook the nation. Looting and rioting and images of the National Guard using tear gas and flash grenades against peaceful protesters will ever be etched in Americans' minds. All of this was topped off by a long and protracted political season that deeply divided us and cast doubt on the strength of our democracy. Indeed, the year 2020 was an earthquake of mass proportions.

Not only were we rocked by the physical, economical, and political shaking, but many were rattled by insurmountable grief and emotional toll. Humanity wept as the COVID death angel claimed the lives of our most beloved. They were our grandparents, best friends, next door neighbors, pastors, teachers, and more. Still, in the backdrop of the virus, life continued. Others who bypassed the virus were lost to other causes unexpectedly. In the crucible of our heartbreak, the heat of anxiety and despair raged. Our faith wavered, and yes, sometimes it failed. Our hope waned, and for some it even expired. Nevertheless, my hope is that as you read *Hope Through the Fire: Winning with the Word and Prayer* that your hope will be revived.

My desire is that you will be reminded that even if you can't see God through the blaze of your fiery furnace, you can still take comfort in knowing that He's always there. Not only standing there with you as Jehovah Shammah but fighting for you as Jehovah Nissi, working both behind the scenes and in front so that this, too, will work together for your good. He alone is our Hope and the unchanging God of Scripture. He is the Rock of Ages and the Ancient of days. Our fires don't catch Him by surprise. The Bible reveals that God has been with His people through unimaginable times before, and so will He be with us. My hope is that as you recall His faithfulness and connect with Him through prayer, this book will help you to trust Him.

<u>Crises in Health</u>
"Beloved, I wish above all things that thou mayest prosper and be in good health, even as thou soul prospereth."
- 3 John 1:2

Not Without a Fight

2 Kings 20:1-11

Turn again, and tell Hezekiah the captain of my people, Thus saith the Lord, the God of David thy father, I have heard thy prayer, I have seen thy tears: behold, I will heal thee: on the third day thou shalt go up unto the house of the Lord. - 2 Kings 20:5

When King Hezekiah was told by the Prophet Isaiah that he would die from a severe illness, he immediately petitioned God for a different result. Nevermind that the Prophet Isaiah was a well-respected man of God whose prophecies included the birth and crucifixion of the coming Messiah. Hezekiah refused to allow the prophet's integrity and spiritual pedigree to bar him from seeking another report from God himself. Scripture informs us that before Isaiah could leave the king's court, God directed him to turn around and give Hezekiah another, more favorable report. King Hezekiah would not die but live--for 15 more years, in fact. Not only would God extend his life, but He promised to defend the king's city from imminent attack. That was a blessing Hezekiah didn't ask for and a testament to the power of audacious prayer.

Maybe you're like King Hezekiah and you've received a bad report. Maybe it's terminal cancer, six months to live, mental illness with a lifetime of harmful medication, or worse. What we learn from the king is that no matter how credible the bearer of bad news is or how formidable the disease may be, we can refuse to resign ourselves to an unwanted fate. The Great Physician still has the final say, and we have influence with Him. Hezekiah reminded the Lord of his service to Him, and we can be sure that our faithfulness to the Lord carries weight too. Even if we haven't been as consistent in our charity and godly character, we can still appeal to God on the basis that we are His children. Our Father is concerned about what concerns us. Our desperation does not repulse Him. No matter how many times we may have petitioned Him before, a "yes" is still possible. Summon the courage to approach Him one more time. God is the God of miracles.

Winning with Prayer

Dear Heavenly Father,

Thank You for the privilege to boldly approach Your throne. Your compassion is endless, and You always hear the cries of Your people. I know that my situation seems hopeless, but You are able to turn things around for me. I humble myself to petition You again about my situation, and I trust You will work all things together for my good. In Jesus' name. Amen.

Against the Odds
Mark 5:25-34

When she had heard of Jesus, [she] came in the press behind, and touched his garment. For she said, If I may touch but his clothes, I shall be whole. - Mark 5:27-28

The woman with the issue of blood's illness was so severe and personal that the Bible doesn't give her ailment or her name; yet, her sickness was a matter of public discourse. For 12 years, her trickling blood and resultant stench announced her body's revolt and signaled her imminent death. Every physician, healer, and religious leader knew her; however, none had been able to offer a cure. Indeed, the best of religion, science, and medicine had only made her worse. Nevertheless, the bleeding woman refused to resign herself to a bad prognosis. She remained expectant that her deliverance was coming despite the years of suffering she'd endured. Just hearing of the miracles Jesus had done for others made her resolute that He could do the same for her – even if He didn't speak to her or touch her. She knew a miraculous breakthrough was on the way.

A medical miracle for you or your loved one is possible too. There are no incurable illnesses with God, and even terminal diseases meet expiration dates when Jesus is involved. Like the bleeding woman with indomitable faith, we must maintain a steadfast determination that Jesus can heal us no matter how long it's been, who's told us we'll never be set free, or how much we've lost. We must press into God's presence and resist the urge to shrink back in defeat. We must press past the cancer diagnosis. Press past HIV/AIDS. Jesus is in the room. All hope is not lost. What He's done for others, He can do for us. We must believe.

Winning with Prayer

Dear Heavenly Father,

Thank You that nothing is too hard for You! You have power over sickness, disease, and our most debilitating disappointments. You alone have the final say. Fill me with the faith to believe that when I press into Your presence I can be forever changed and set free. Let my life bear witness that by the stripes of Jesus I am healed and made whole by the power of His blood. In Jesus' name. Amen.

Beyond Excuses
John 5:2-9

When Jesus saw him lie, and knew that he had been now a long time in that case, he saith unto him, Wilt thou be made whole? - John 5:6

Life often throws us curve balls that not only hit us but take us out of the game. We may physically recover and even attempt to resume our normal activities, but our zest for life, our belief in ourselves, and our passion to pursue our dreams may be permanently derailed. That was the state of the man Jesus met near the pool of Bethsaida. The man's body had nursed his infirmity for 38 years, and he was only one of a host of incapacitated people to throng the area in hopes that they could be healed. It was believed that if one was first to step into the pool after it was troubled by an angel then one's health would be restored. The man, who was lame, had come to the pool for years and never been first in the water. While the man likely lamented over the decades spent in pain and frustration, it was those 38 years that garnered the mercy of Christ. Without being prodded, Jesus had observed the man and offered him the opportunity to be made whole. After years of being overlooked, stepped on, and pushed, the man was now before the Great Physician, about to be healed spontaneously; yet, all he had was excuses.

How many times do we allow an illness or handicap to become a crutch? So many times we resign ourselves to living beneath our potential or dealing with an unhealthy situation even when we know God's promises. We must remember that our God is the God of hope. He is the God whose plans for each of us are good (Jeremiah 29:11). Whether we wait one day or nearly 40 years, we must believe that God can change our situations just as He did for the infirmed man. Further, we must believe that He is able to heal us and change our situations spontaneously, regardless if we're deserving or qualified. Healing doesn't always have to come the way we expected but we have to trust that it will come.

Winning with Prayer
Dear Heavenly Father,

Thank You for being a merciful and compassionate God. Thank You that even when I give up on myself or deem my situation hopeless, You never give up on me. You see past my excuses, look beyond my faults, and dismiss my doubt to bless me anyway. You pity me as a father does his son. Because You love me, I know that it's never too late to be healed. In Jesus' name. Amen.

Personal Struggles

"Search me, O God, and know my heart: try me, and know my thoughts: And see if there be any wicked way in me, and lead me in the way everlasting."
- Psalm 139:23-24

Lord, Fix My Heart
Luke 18:35-43

And they which went before rebuked him, that he should hold his peace: but he cried so much the more, Thou Son of David, have mercy on me. - Luke 18:39

Seeing is believing, or so the saying goes, but the story of Bartimaeus, a blind beggar near the town of Jericho, shows us otherwise. He is called by his disability and largely dismissed by the crowds following Jesus until he erupts into uncommon praise. The blind man seems to be the only person who can see that he is in the presence of the Savior because he is the only one greeting Jesus with worship. While many in the crowd attempt to quiet Bartimaeus, the Savior is arrested by his praise and demands that members of the crowd bring him to Jesus. Jesus graciously fulfills Bartimaeus' request to have his sight restored, and the whole crowd glorifies God along with the once blind man.

Sometimes it takes that one person who is on fire for God to reveal our stagnation and lack of passion for the God who saved us from our sins. Bartimaeus' fervent worship revealed the seeing crowd's blindness toward the God who is worthy of praise and who chose to grace them with His presence. Their content to walk with Him in silence and shush someone who actually understood that God deserves to be worshipped speaks volumes about the quality of the crowd's relationship with God. It speaks volumes about their state of mind. It speaks volumes about the condition of their hearts. Perhaps your relationship has been this way too – following God without lauding Him, walking with Him without getting to know Him, and failing to understand or serve His purpose or His people. The truth is that at any time any of us could find ourselves in this place. I certainly have. It's the place where we're comfortable but not intimate. It's the place where it takes a miracle of God to bring us back into awe and wonder at who He is. It can feel like a prison until you break free.

So how do we get there? How do we break free? We must first thank God for making us aware of the problem. Oftentimes the numbness we feel when we're out of communion with God is His beckoning for us to go deeper in fellowship. What we learn from Bartimaeus is that we can reignite our fire by simply praising God for who He is. We can allow our faith in Him to be an act of worship. We can think of the testimonies and miracles He's already performed in our own lives and worship Him with our gratitude. We can be persistent, persevering even when it seems we're not getting through. As long as we keep our testimonies close to our hearts, we can overcome our struggles with apathy and draw closer to the Lover of our souls.

Winning with Prayer
Dear Heavenly Father,

Thank You for the nearness of You. You are nearer than my breath even when You seem so far away. There is nothing that can separate me from Your amazing love. Help me to be closer to You. Have my heart. Restore me to deeper fellowship with You as I seek You through devotion, prayer, and praise. In Jesus' name. Amen.

Thirsty No More
John 4:1-30

But whosoever drinketh of the water that I shall give him shall never thirst; but the water that I shall give him shall be in him a well of water springing up into everlasting life. - John 4:14

It's been said that sin takes you farther than you want to go and keeps you longer than you wanted to stay. Sin is bondage, and there doesn't seem to be a greater stronghold than the mire of sexual sin. In 1 Corinthians 6:18, the Apostle Paul wisely admonishes us all to flee fornication. Not walk, not run, but *flee*. During Christ's exchange with a Samaritan woman at a well in her town, the conversation moves from a discussion of physical thirst to a spiritual one when Jesus mentions she is entangled in sexual sin. Specifically, He tells her about the number of sexual partners she's had and reveals her current situation (another relationship with a married man). The woman is caught in a cycle that has a spiritual root, but she can only focus on the physical need until Jesus offers her His living water. Suddenly, she is set free from her shame and released to free others.

It would be easy to dismiss the Samaritan woman's struggles with illicit sex as promiscuity, but as with most addictions, there were likely deeper reasons. Bad advice for pretty girls. Childhood sexual abuse. More. Like those who wrestle with addictions such as drug and alcohol dependencies or gambling, the Samaritan woman was trapped in a dysfunction that was bigger than her. Maybe even that didn't begin with her. Over the years, she had tried at least five times to break free with no success. Only when she talked with Jesus and allowed Him to minister to her brokenness could she be made whole.

Just as He was the solution for the woman of Samaria, Jesus is the answer for us too. The world offers us counseling, therapy, and rehabilitation, but they are incomplete. Without God's Word and consistent prayer, the strongholds in our lives can never be imploded. We must have honest talks with Jesus. Tell Him about the urges. Tell Him about the desires. He knows already. Leave your shame behind and receive His living water. God is waiting with acceptance and love without condemnation.

Winning with Prayer
Dear Heavenly Father,

Thank You for Your grace and mercy poured out just for me. I know that I cannot overcome my temptations or the strongholds I face by myself. I need Your help. I accept Your living water. Trade my desires for Your desires. Be strength for my weakness as I seek to live in freedom, health, and love. In Jesus' name. Amen.

__Family__
"Can a mother forget the baby at her breast and have no compassion on the child she has borne? Though she may forget, I will not forget you! See, I have engraved you on the palms of my hands; your walls are ever before me."
- Isaiah 49:15-16 NIV

A Love That Saves

Genesis 18:16-33

And [Abraham] said, Oh let not the LORD be angry, and I will speak yet but this once: Peradventure ten shall be found there. And [God] said, I will not destroy it for ten's sake. - Genesis 18:32

The story of Abraham pleading with God for the salvation of the morally bankrupt city of Sodom is one of enduring family love. Abraham's nephew, Lot, the son of his beloved and deceased brother, pitched his tent near the city. Sodom was so rampant with sin that its decadence roused the concern of God. Abraham and others were aware of God's impending judgement on Sodom, but the others turned away. Instead Abraham stood with God, appealing to His mercy and His heart for all of His people. After acknowledging his mere humanity in the presence of the holy, Almighty God, Abraham proceeded to ask God to save the city if He found as little as ten righteous people. God agreed.

So many times we see our family members in imminent danger, and we wonder what we can do. Many of them are unsaved or have feeble relationships with the Lord. They may not know or appreciate the power of prayer of fasting, and they may need a more mature person to intercede for them. God just may have assigned them the problem so you or someone in their circle could intercede for the larger community or even the world. We must have enough love, hope, and faith to believe that our prayers and intercession can make a difference with God. God's heart is that none should perish but that all should come to repentance (2 Peter 3:9). We cannot be discouraged by His initial adverse pronouncements when we know the bend of His heart. The fate of your loved one's soul (and others) could depend on it.

Winning with Prayer
Dear Heavenly Father,

Thank You for the love You have for my family. You hear my earnest pleas and petitions on their behalf. You know all about the tough situations my loved ones are dealing with, and Your arm is mighty to save them. Do it for Your glory in Jesus' name. Amen.

Bad Blood

Genesis 25:20-34 and 27:1-45

And he said, Is not he rightly named Jacob? for he hath supplanted me these two times: he took away my birthright; and, behold, now he hath taken away my blessing. [...] - Genesis 27:36

Even in the womb, younger twin Jacob was after older twin Esau. The younger brother would go on to take advantage of his elder's impatience and natural craving for food to secure his birthright. He maliciously deceived his father into giving him the blessing exclusively reserved for the firstborn. To say he was manipulative and selfish is an understatement. Expectedly, his behavior drove a wedge between him and his twin and damaged his family. Jacob even had to flee the house permanently to escape from Esau's anger. His family would never be the same.

Indeed, the destruction to Jacob's family seemed beyond repair. Nevertheless, the wonderful thing about God is that no matter how devastating and complicated our family histories and dynamics are, He can always bring a peaceful reconciliation. It would take years of Jacob working for his uncle (who was also his father-in-law) for God to develop the humility, honor, and respect Jacob needed to apologize to Esau. Their reunion was 20 years in the making, but it happened. When they finally came together again, the scathing anger Esau had was replaced with nothing but love.

Do you have family members you haven't spoken to in a while because of a major disagreement, abuse, or some other catastrophic reason? Do you think the damage is irreversible and the differences irreconcilable? Let me remind you that there's nothing too hard for God. It's okay to hope for reconciliation and peace even after the toughest of fallouts. God can heal calloused hearts. God can bind gunshot wounds. He specializes in brokenness. If there's an ember of hope in you for reconciliation, then it may be an urging from God telling you it's time. Pray about it and then see what next steps He may want you to take. Your family may not come back together, but at least you both can have peace.

Winning with Prayer
Dear Heavenly Father,

Thank You for being the Mender of broken hearts. You know the depth of the pain I feel about my loved one, and only You can make it right. I call out to You now for the strength and courage to forgive what I may never be able to forget. I ask You to help me become Your minister of reconciliation and healing in my personal sphere even as I commit to doing so in the world. In Jesus' name. Amen.

Mama Wounds
Matthew 14:3-11

So she, having been prompted by her mother, said, "Give me John the Baptist's head here on a platter."
- Matthew 14:8

"Father hurt" is well publicized whether we speak of absentee fathers, abusive fathers, or overbearing fathers. Indeed, men receive their fair share of the blame for poor parenting, but mothers can hurt their children too. The pain can be equally, if not more, devastating when one considers the special relationship between a mother and her child. One of the most endearing relationships a mother can have is with her daughter. A mother teaches her daughter how to be nurturing and empathetic, how to build up others, and how to make a home. Sadly, however, this is not always the case.

The Bible tells the story of a mother-daughter duo, King Herod's wife Herodias and her daughter. The queen desired the head of John the Baptist and used her daughter to influence Herod to have the prophet killed. Specifically, the mother encouraged the daughter to dance provocatively before the king and his guests, such that the king promised to give her anything she wanted. Instead of helping her daughter to give life, King Herod's wife trained her to be an assassin. Instead of teaching her princess to respect her body, the queen taught her to use her physical assets to manipulate men for her benefit, even if it meant incest. There probably wasn't a low this mother wouldn't encourage her daughter to cross. Imagine the hurts she must've masked and the scars she carried as a result.

Many women don't have to imagine her pain because their story is similar. Maybe you know one of them. Maybe you are one of them. You have trouble trusting women. You can't respect men. You manipulate everyone in your life to get things you want. You violate your body. Sound familiar? All of these things are logs of a spiritual fire that's blazing out of control, but God is the ultimate firefighter. He's also a wonderful Counselor who can heal you. He's not just Abba Father, but He's Mother to the motherless. He's better than any physical mother you could ever have, and He knows all about your issues. Give Him your heart.

Winning with Prayer

Dear Heavenly Father,

Thank You for knowing the complexities of my childhood and of my innermost being. Thank You for caring about the hurts I've endured even at the hands of the one who gave life to me. Today, I choose not to be a motherless child. I declare that You mother me. I lay my head in Your bosom to be held close by the perfect Parent and receive the perfect love. Help me to trust again. Help me to forgive. Heal my memories and teach me what I wasn't taught. I know that You can. In Jesus' name. Amen.

Lord, Have Mercy

2 Samuel 13:1-19

And she answered him, Nay, my brother, do not force me, for no such thing ought to be done in Israel: do not thou this folly. - 2 Samuel 13:12

What would you do? What would you say? Most people would be angry and maybe even retaliate if they learned their daughter had been sexually violated. The pain would be especially acute if the violator was your own son, the victim's brother. How would you protect your daughter? How would you go about exacting justice? How would you go about forgiving? How could you go to God?

King David once faced a situation like this one. His precious, virgin daughter Tamar was raped by her brother Amnon in the palace. This act was so completely heinous that David couldn't give words or action to his anger. The Bible doesn't even specifically record what his words were to God about the matter. David was so shocked that he did nothing. Tamar would be avenged by her brother Absalom who would take matters into his own hands. He would conspire to kill Amnon and then attempt to kill David too. Absalom would later be murdered. All of this violence and loss of life took place because of the diabolical act and David's failure to offer discipline to his son or get help for his daughter.

Unfortunately, the incest Tamar experienced is not uncommon. Sadly, similar violations occur with far too many young people throughout their childhood. The

Centers for Disease Control reported in their "Preventing Childhood Sexual Abuse" that "[a]bout 1 in 4 girls and 1 in 13 boys experience child sexual abuse at some point in childhood" and that "91% of child sexual abuse is perpetrated by someone the child or child's family knows." Lord, have mercy! We must be careful with our children, even when they're under our roof. Even when they're with our friends and relatives. Even when they're with our other children. If any of us finds ourselves in the situation David faced as a parent, we must ask God for the wisdom and the anointing to deal with each child with love considering each child's needs. We must be led to the Rock that is higher than we are. He is the only Answer, the only Solution. Our hope is that He will hear our prayers, mend our families, and make us stronger than we were before.

Winning with Prayer
Dear Heavenly Father,

Thank You, Lord, that You never leave or forsake me even when the most unexpected, horrific events happen in my family. You are as much with me during the bad days as You are during the good. Father, when I want to lose my mind in anger or rage, give me Your peace that surpasses understanding. Help me to treat each family member with love and resolve challenging matters with Your godly wisdom. Anoint my words and help me know what to say. Direct my actions so I'll be led by You. Heal us. Fix us. Put us back together. Help my children to be more than statistics. Restore their self-esteem and self-image. Don't let them have the wrong desires. Help them to trust again. Put legions of angels all around them to guide every step so they are safe. In Jesus' name. Amen.

Romance

"The things which are impossible with men are possible with God." - Luke 18:27

Entangled

2 Samuel 11:1 - 12:19

Then David sent messengers to get her. She came to him, and he slept with her. - 2 Samuel 11:4a NIV

David heard that Bathsheba was married to another man, but it went in one ear and out the other. Her naked beauty had captivated him, and he wanted her. With every fiber of his being. Forget that he had beautiful wives at home. Forget that the God he worshipped and adored expressly forbade adultery. His desire had been aroused. He had to have her, even if it was only for a night. Perhaps these were the thoughts that drove David to seize her, make love to her, and send her home...pregnant. Try as he might, he couldn't trick her husband, the honorable Uriah, into sleeping with his wife so that the baby would be considered his. Thus, in an act of desperation, David arranged to have Uriah killed so he could marry his pregnant wife. Ain't it just scandalous?!

Maybe you're a man or woman of God who's found yourself in the quagmire of lust. It could be an extramarital affair, an entanglement, or a situationship where you've allowed your lower members to overrule what you know is right in your head and heart. Before it goes any further, before anyone else gets hurt – stop! Repent and ask God for forgiveness. You don't have to let unbridled passion have control of you. And if you've only entertained the idea of consummating your lust but not acted on your thoughts, take this as your confirmation that you shouldn't do it. The Bible says that adultery begins in the heart and that even looking at someone with lust causes sin (Matthew 5:28). David's lust not only cost an innocent man his life but cost the life of David and Bathsheba's child. Think that's severe? Well, it didn't end there. God further punished David by allowing strife in his family that led to the violation of his daughter and the death of other sons. Trust me, his momentary pleasure was not worth the pain, and neither is yours. Sexual attraction does not have to lead to sex. God is able to help you take control of illicit desires no matter how strong. Don't give up hope that He has someone specifically for you that you won't have to share.

Winning with Prayer
Dear Heavenly Father,

Thank You for Your unfailing love that washes away my sins. Lord, I want to live a life that is pure and God-pleasing, but I feel so overwhelmed by my desires. Help me to mortify the deeds of my flesh and follow after Your Spirit. Help me to withstand temptation and take the way of escape You have made for me. In Jesus' name. Amen.

Save Me

Genesis 29:16-34; 49:29-31

And when the LORD saw that Leah was hated, he opened her womb: but Rachel was barren. - Genesis 29:31

Having babies doesn't make a husband love his wife, but sometimes, it's the last resort of a woman who's desperately starved for her husband's attention and affection. Leah was Jacob's first wife, but his heart had always belonged to his second wife, Rachel. Rachel just happened to be Leah's younger, more attractive sister. It was Rachel Jacob kissed the very first time he met her. It was Rachel Jacob had worked for seven years to marry only to discover Leah in the bridal bed. It was Rachel Jacob had agreed to work for another seven years after being duped. Leah had simply been a pawn in her father's game to get more work out of Jacob. That Leah would expect Jacob to love her as his wife when she had witnessed how committed he was to Rachel is both incredible and unreasonable. Nevertheless, God moved in her favor when He saw that His beloved daughter was hated by the man she loved. God opened her womb and left Rachel barren for many years. Despite this and six children from Leah, Jacob's heart remained calloused toward his first wife. Upon giving birth to her last child, the weary wife named her son Judah in acknowledgment of learning to set her affections on the Lord.

While Leah may have given up on her desire of having a place in Jacob's heart, God did not. Rachel's untimely death gave Leah years with Jacob all to herself. While the Bible doesn't say he became smitten with his remaining wife, it doesn't record that he looked for another spouse (though he had the means to do so). When Leah died, Jacob honored her by burying her beside his ancestors, the great patriarchs and matriarchs of Israel.

God can turn around even the most fragile of unions. No matter the level of dysfunction, God can restore order. No matter how long one spouse has had a wandering heart, God can still knit the two hearts He joined together so no man can put them asunder. If your marriage is in turmoil, don't lose hope. Begin to praise God like Leah, and watch God show up strong in your situation. He may not come when you want Him, but He will show up when you need Him! He has a plan for your union. Don't give up!

<u>Winning with Prayer</u>
Dear Heavenly Father,

Thank You that when I've come to the end of my rope in my marriage, You are able to hold us together in spite of it all. Thank You for seeing the depth of my deepest pain and answering my "impossible" prayers. Thank You for being the Third Strand in our marriage cord. In Jesus's name. Amen.

Loss

"And I will restore to you the years that the locust hath eaten, the cankerworm, and the caterpillar, and the palmerworm, my great army which I sent among you. And ye shall eat in plenty, and be satisfied, and praise the name of the LORD your God, that hath dealt wondrously with you: and my people shall never be ashamed."
- Joel 2:25-26

Down But Not Out

1 Samuel 30:1-19

And David was greatly distressed; for the people spake of stoning him, because the soul of all the people was grieved, every man for his sons and for his daughters: but David encouraged himself in the Lord his God.
- 1 Samuel 30:6

In 1 Samuel 30, David and his men discover that their wives and children were taken captive by a rival army. The men weep bitterly and eventually talk of stoning their leader. While the embattled king could've retreated in fear, the Bible says in 1 Samuel 30:6 that "David encouraged himself in the Lord his God."

Sometimes life can be so debilitating and full of unpleasant surprises that you want to hide. We lose loved ones unexpectedly and beyond our control. People charged with protecting us and those fighting with us suddenly turn against us. It's in these times that we must remember we have hope in the Lord who is for us when all are against us. Instead of resigning ourselves to defeat or self-pity, we must lean on our faith. We must remember that we are beloved children of the Most High God. We must remember that God only allows pain for His divine purpose.

David's faith in God was rewarded. His prayer was answered favorably. He wasn't stoned. The wives and children were ultimately recovered unharmed. Remain in faith when it seems all hope is lost. God is the God of restoration who can help you recover it all, so don't worry about the mistakes you've made. Don't worry about the money you've wasted. God's going to "open up the window of Heaven and pour you out a blessing you won't have room enough to receive" (Malachi 3:10). Don't fret about the time you spent with the wrong people. God's going to redeem the time and "repay you for the years the locusts have eaten" (Joel 2:25). Don't shrink back from your losses. With God's blessing, go after what was taken from you. Get your joy back, pursue your peace, take the steps to restore your relationships, and more. Refuse to die before God calls you. Refuse to go down without a fight. Let the losses in your life reveal the indomitable champion in you. God made you to win, so show them what a winner looks like.

Winning with Prayer
Dear Heavenly Father,

Thank You for being my Rock and my Redeemer. You collect all of my tears in Your cup and repurpose them for Your glory. Regardless of the mistakes I make, You are always on my side. Help me to take back all that the enemy has stolen from me, for You alone are my Restorer. Help me to remain in faith as You work behind the scenes to rebuild me in Jesus' name. Amen.

Life After Death

Ruth 1

I went out full and the Lord hath brought me home again empty[...]. - Ruth 1:21

First, she lost her husband, then God took her two sons. Surely, Naomi knew what it meant to grieve. Her pain was so intense that this loving, God-fearing woman whose name meant "pleasant" desired that her name be changed to Mara, which means "bitterness." Upon returning to her native land, she told her people that the Lord had emptied, afflicted, and dealt harshly with her.

Maybe you've endured the sudden death of a loved one you held dear. Maybe it wasn't the death of a person but the dissolution of a marriage, a traumatic breakup, the dashing of long-held dreams, the foreclosure of a home or a business that made you feel as if God had dealt you a bad hand. Maybe you think the pain and heartbreak will never end, and you don't mind telling anyone who'll listen. Well, I've got news for you: God can handle your disappointment. It's not like He doesn't already know all about it and your feelings. He is our High Priest who is touched by our infirmities despite being sinless (Hebrews 4:15). When God invites us to cast our cares on Him, He does so from a place of empathy because He is also acquainted with many sorrows and grief (Isaiah 53:3).

Despite the heartbreak in our lives, God ultimately desires that our joy be fulfilled (John 17:13). We may never understand the whys, but we can believe that better days are ahead, and we can take stock of what we do have. Naomi still had Ruth. Because God kept Ruth in Naomi's life, Naomi had purpose after her grief. It was Naomi who coached Ruth on how to approach Boaz, who would become their kinsmen redeemer. It was Naomi who became nurse to Ruth's child, Obed, who was the grandfather of King David and an ancestor to King Jesus.

How will God restore you? How will He use the people who remain in your life to rebuild you? Stay hopeful because when God is in it there will always be glory after major disappointment. Don't let the tears blind you to who Jesus is. He never changes. He's always loving, always concerned about you, always praying for you, always in your corner. There *will* be breakthrough. You *will* smile again. Believe it.

Winning with Prayer
Dear Heavenly Father,

Thank You for being intimately acquainted with my grief. Thank You that I can be honest about my emotions and my pain, for You are my closest friend. Help me to believe that my weeping will be followed with joy. In Jesus' name, I pray. Amen.

Redeemed
Isaiah 54

O thou afflicted, tossed with tempest, and not comforted, behold, I will lay thy stones with fair colours, and lay thy foundations with sapphires. - Isaiah 54:11

Isaiah 54 tells the story of God consoling a heartbroken woman whose barrenness is the result of her sinful marriage to youthful folly. Her "marriage" of the wrong men had made her a widow, yet her "husband" had given her no lasting fruit to show of their union. She was left only to bear the shame and reproach of not bearing children when everyone knew she had been fruitful. While the men she had cavorted with hadn't regarded her as worthy of an honorable marriage, God had always esteemed her as His precious bride. As such, He counted her sin – indeed, her betrayal – as egregious as the world's sins that merited the great flood. In addition to her physical impotence, He allowed affliction and debilitating storms where she was forsaken by Him. She was so disappointed by the loss of her dreams that she was afraid to dream again, to hope again, or believe that God would comfort her again. Nevertheless, God assured her that His anger was temporary and that He would overwhelm her with kindness, mercy, and peace. He told her that He had called her to be a wife from her youth even while she was forsaken and that He would redeem her to her place of royalty, which is how He had seen her. Her fears would not be realized, though she would see them form. She had suffered enough. Her pain was over. She was redeemed.

Perhaps there were mistakes you made in your youth that have compromised the quality of life you live in your adulthood. You kept giving your heart to the wrong people. You kept allowing the wrong friends into your life. You kept making the

the wrong choices with alcohol and drugs. However sinful ways have halted your life, you can have hope that God's anger lasts only a little while but His mercy endures forever. God says that your suffering is over now. It's your time to be what He ordained you to be from the beginning. Sure, that doesn't mean that you won't face people who won't be happy about the favor on your life. They will form weapons at your sanity, your happiness, and your productivity, but none of them will prosper against you. The Maker of Heaven and earth is for you and more than the whole world against you (Romans 8:31)! Walk out of the shadow of who you used to be and walk into your new season. You are redeemed!

Winning with Prayer
Dear Heavenly Father,

Thank You for being my Redeemer. You see value in me where I and others have only counted me as worthless. You resurrect my hopes and dreams. You help me live the life You imagined for me. Thank You for not changing Your mind about me despite my sins. Help me to see myself as You see me and make the choices that won't grieve Your heart. In Jesus' name. Amen.

<u>Church</u>

"There is one body, and one Spirit, even as ye are called in one hope of your calling; One Lord, one faith, one baptism, One God and Father of all, who is above all, and through all, and in you all." - Ephesians 4:4-6

Down to My Last Dime
Luke 20:46-47; Luke 21:1-4

And he said, Of a truth I say unto you, that this poor widow hath cast in more than they all: For all these have of their abundance cast in unto the offerings of God: but she of her penury hath cast in all the living that she had.
- Luke 21:3-4

Did you know that not all of the people who attend church regularly are frequent givers? In fact, most church attenders are not. According to Nonprofit Source's 2018 Charitable Giving Statistics, Trends & Data Charitable Giving for Churches, tithers make up only 10%-25% of the congregation. According to the same statistics, 80% of the congregation gives only 2% of its income. When we consider that tithing is a commandment of God, both in the new and old testaments of the Holy Bible, then we can see how short the Gospel has come to converting our hearts. Furthermore, when we consider the poor widow who gave all she had when those with more material resources gave insubstantially based on how God had blessed them, then we can see that most of us really have far to go when it comes to worshipping the Lord through giving.

For those who do bless the Lord with 10% of their earnings and an offering, it can be understandable how they could feel slighted and underappreciated by leaders who seem to discount their sacrifices or shamefully ask for more. Many of them not only contribute financially but also serve with their time and talents. They are aware of their significant contributions and the integral roles they play in serving the Lord and His church. They are also aware of how others who don't participate meaningfully downplay their contributions. Nevertheless, they continue to give and serve undergirded by their great love for God.

The poor widow woman who cast her only two mites into the collection plate one day was one such giver. No doubt she was aware of the wealthy men whose contributions were much less of a sacrifice to them than hers. She'd probably listened to some of them minister to her and the congregation about sacrificial giving knowing that they didn't practice what they preached. They didn't have her bills. They didn't have her very limited income. They knew her strain, though, and still pressured her in the name of the Lord. Their motives weren't a secret to her, but she gave anyway. She gave anyway because her love for God and faith in Him were greater than the pain of betrayal by her brothers in the faith.

I want this to be your story. I want you to move past the abuse (financial or otherwise) that you've experienced in your house of worship and not allow it to make you give up on God or the body of Christ. I know that may be a big hope. You may be wondering how God could allow them to get away with what they're doing. You may wonder how those who are supposed to be examples could be wolves in sheep's clothing. Well, God sees them, and He sees you. Like he did with the widow woman, God is using you as a lesson to show His leaders what true devotion and sincerity look like. He may decide to remove you from the situation, or He may not. Either way, keep your eye on God. Move when He says move and not a minute before. He will give you the grace to stay in the heat if that's what He's told you.

Giver, God has promised you that the windows of Heaven are open to you. The enemy of your soul is rebuked for your sake. Your life is filled to overflowing with blessings, many of which will flow to generations of your family and community such that your people won't be able to handle them all! All because you give. Remember that all blessings aren't visible to the naked eye. We know that they're there even when we can't see them because God's Word doesn't lie. Continue to sow your seeds of faith as The Holy Spirit leads. There *will* be a harvest.

Winning with Prayer
Dear Heavenly Father,

Thank You for being a giving God. You are the giver of every good and perfect gift, and all that I have flows from You. Thank You for blessing me to return a portion to You and support the work of Your kingdom. I know that You honor the sacrifices I make and will bless me according to Your Word. Help me to pray for those who lack my level of commitment or who try to take advantage of my heart. Restore the joy of giving and help me to remain faithful and cheerful in attitude and obedience. In Jesus' name. Amen.

Drowning in Shame
John 8:1-11

And Jesus said unto her, Neither do I condemn thee: go, and sin no more. - John 8:11

As if falling in love with another woman's husband wasn't bad enough, the woman who stood before Jesus had been accosted by religious leaders in the middle of sexual relations! While they had permitted her lover to escape, they had paraded her naked through the town en route to the synagogue where they hoped Jesus would consent to her being stoned. This wouldn't be the only time religious people would attempt to get God's approval to commit a worse sin than that of the person they were looking to punish. In the past, women seeking abortions were killed by religious zealots hellbent on punishing those who murder the innocent without considering that all life is precious to God. Two wrongs have never made a right, and "all have sinned and fallen short of His glory" (Romans 3:23). When Jesus reminds the religious leaders that only God is in a position to judge, they abandon their plans to take the woman's life. And though God could mete judgement for her sin, He grants her mercy and pardons her instead.

Unfortunately, there are too many instances where those charged with shepherding the flock of God have only condemned when they should've shown the unconditional love of Christ. If you've found yourself in a similar situation, I want you to know that God sees your pain. He wants you to know that you can never make a mistake that He can't forgive. He wants you to know that He can deal with the religious leaders who hurt you. He's their God too. They hurt you because they were immature and didn't understand His love for themselves. You don't have to exact revenge or walk away from church completely. Let Him heal you. He will build you back up. He will build you back up. He will restore your self-respect and vindicate your name.

Winning with Prayer

Dear Heavenly Father,

Thank You for Your compassion that looks beyond my sin. I know that I've disappointed You and that I don't even deserve to be alive. Thank You for preserving my life with Your love. Help me to sin no more. In Jesus' name, I pray. Amen.

Even Me
Galatians 4:12-16

And my temptation which was in my flesh ye despised not, nor rejected; but received me as an angel of God, even as Christ Jesus. – Galatians 4:14

Many of us love our pastors and spiritual leaders. They are the ones who reveal the heart of God to us and the ones who provide comfort to us during life's most challenging times. We celebrate them for the examples God allows them to be in spite of their known faults and shortcomings; however, many parishioners would abandon their leaders if they were aware of their secret struggles. Because they believe they must be perfect for the people, many spiritual leaders are dangerously depressed and some live double lives. The unconditional love they give by not judging hurting parishioners for their faults and strongholds is often not reciprocated though everyone needs grace.

This double standard is well known, but the Bible offers an example of a congregation that wraps its arms around the pastor while fully aware of his struggle. The pastor was the Apostle Paul, and the congregation was the church at Galatia. The Apostle Paul was renowned for his piety and command of Holy Scripture, yet God revealed to this church his tempting "infirmity of the flesh" (Galatians 4:13). Instead of responding with gossip, ridicule, and repudiation, the Galatian church responded with mercy, acceptance, and love. Paul said they still treated him as "an angel" and the mouthpiece of Christ. So great was their affection toward him that they would've given him whatever he needed despite their awareness of his private affliction (Galatians 4:14-15). How comforting for the undershepherds to know that not only can the love they give can be reciprocated but that love can be mature! Love can cover. Love can protect. Love can look for the best in the beloved even when the worst stares back at her. We must recognize our own humanity and in turn make allowances for it in others.

Pastoral leaders and ministers, like those they serve, are imperfect humans striving to imitate the perfect God. There will be mistakes. There will be gross shortcomings. Great people often have great flaws. Expect spiritual battles that they will sometimes lose. The same is true for all of us. As God's Spirit is poured out on all flesh in these last days, there will be those whose discernment is keen to recognize even the secret struggles and frailties of their leaders. You may be one of them. Such knowledge should be met with prayer. Such knowledge must be tempered with compassion and mercy, for the same devil that seeks to kill, steal, and destroy you is the same one after your leaders. Even the pastor needs the grace they preach about. Everyone benefits when love and acceptance flow freely in the house of God. This is the pathway to unity, joy, and peace. Let it start with you.

Winning with Prayer
Dear Heavenly Father,

Thank You for loving community and fellowship. Thank You for the leaders You have given to me after Your own heart. As they shepherd my family and our community, help us to accept each other's strengths and weaknesses with honor and respect. In Jesus' name, we pray. Amen.

Yes, Lord

Acts 9:10-18

Then Ananias answered, Lord, I have heard by many of this man, how much evil he hath done to thy saints at Jerusalem: And here he hath authority from the chief priests to bind all that call on thy name. - Acts 9:13-14

God speaks to Ananias about ministering to Saul, who would later be known as the Apostle Paul. Ananias originally has reservations and questions God's command given Saul's history of persecuting Christians. In fact, Ananias reminds God that Saul had even gotten authority to persecute them currently. Helping Saul could very much cost Ananias his life. He could've easily allowed fear and animosity to deter his aid to this future giant of the faith. Instead, he trusted God and helped Saul receive his sight.

So many times in the body of Christ our obedience is the key to someone else's breakthrough, but oftentimes we forget or choose to ignore it because of our own discomfort. God may require us to talk to the person we dislike. God may have us to give up our limited time or money. He may require a change in our lifestyle, and sometimes, He may even require our lives. Ananias was able to do what few would've done because he talked to God first. He wasn't afraid to ask God for clarity. He wasn't afraid to put what was best for God's kingdom above what was best for him personally. Ananias wasn't afraid to answer the call.

God never promised us a life without tribulation; in fact, He promised the contrary. As the people of God, the hope is that everyone will answer God's call regardless of the personal cost. Many disciples face persecution of some kind – why not you? Why not me? The hope is that we will muster courage to become less self-absorbed to care about the people Christ died to save. Even if they were the ones persecuting Him. Even if they persecute us. We must all move past our comfort zones to love as Christ taught us. We must allow God to manifest His Spirit through us so someone else can see. God has prepared them. He's simply waiting for us to move. I believe we can do it. Will you?

Winning with Prayer
Dear Heavenly Father,

Thank You for choosing me to be Your minister. There is no greater privilege than to elected and chosen by You to usher souls into Your kingdom. Help me to push past my fears and prejudices to reach even the most notorious of sinners if You ask me. I want Your glory and Your purposes to be fulfilled through me. Let it be so in Jesus's name. Amen.

__Work__

"Whatever you do, work at it with all your heart, as working for the Lord, not human masters, since you know that you will receive an inheritance from the Lord as a reward. It is the Lord Christ you are serving." - Colossians 3:23-24 NIV

Worth the Risk
Exodus 1:8-21

But the midwives feared God, and did not as the king of Egypt commanded them, but saved the men children alive.
- Exodus 1:17

Many Christians who are passionate believers at church and in their private spheres hide their beliefs at work. It is at work where they are encouraged to remain politically correct and non-confrontational in the interest of being good employees. Usually, this compartmentalized approach to their faith serves them well until a crisis of conscience or some event brings them to a crossroads. For Egyptian midwives Shiprah and Puah, the crisis came from the highest authority of the land. The king of Egypt ordered that all male Hebrew babies be killed because of Egypt's fear of the growing Hebrew slave population. Pharoah did not serve Yahweh or reverence Him, but the midwives did. When faced with the decision to follow the ungodly orders where they would be rewarded by Pharoah or follow the God of their faith, they chose to obey God's law instead of man's. Their decision could've cost them their jobs and even their livelihoods. It could've cost them their lives, but God in His infinite grace protected them. They were questioned by Pharoah, but he didn't exercise judgment against them. Because they feared the Lord more than Pharoah, God blessed them and the Hebrew children were saved.

Whose salvation is dependent on your ability to stand in faith for God when you're confronted with a boss's ungodly demands or expectations? Maybe it's not a matter of salvation. Maybe it's just that your boss or a colleague needs to see that there are still real Christians and people with integrity left. Will you continue to relegate God to the Sunday morning, Wednesday night, five-minute devo God, or will you make the leap to be committed even if it costs you your livelihood? Will you continue to fear Pharoah or the God who made him? Have faith that when you put your hope in God, He will come through. He's the God who makes ways in the deserts and provides rams in the bush. We just have to trust Him. There is a blessing waiting on you that only exists at the end of your ability to take this leap. People who can't speak for themselves are depending on you to advocate for them with your faith. This may not require you to go out of your way to do anything. Perhaps it only requires you to stand.

If you're experiencing a crisis on your job, it could just be that your boss or colleagues need to know that God is higher than themselves. Don't miss the moment for God's glory to shine in your office. If the Holy Spirit is nudging you, push past the worries about what people will think, the what-ifs, and the nerves to do what's right. God is watching. He promises to catch you if you fall.

Winning with Prayer
Dear Heavenly Father,

Thank You for rewarding my obedience and reverence for You with blessings. Give me the confidence to be the same whether I'm at church or at work. Give me the faith to follow You no matter what the consequences are. In Jesus' name, I pray. Amen.

Hater Elevation

Daniel 6

> My God hath sent his angel, and hath shut the lions' mouths, that they have not hurt me: forasmuch as before him innocency was found in me; and also before thee, O king, have I done no hurt. - Daniel 6:22

We must not let the outward circumstances affect us inwardly. This is what we learn from Daniel, the Hebrew that Babylonian King Darius entrusted over his entire kingdom. Daniel had been chosen despite his heritage because of his integrity and excellence. The presidents and princes under him in the kingdom were envious and plotted to use his faith in his God to have him killed. In hopes of killing Daniel, they manipulated King Darius into signing a decree where anyone seeking man or god within 30 days would be thrown into the lion's den. Daniel was aware of the statute but boldly opened his window so his adversaries and anyone else could hear him praying three times a day. Even death wouldn't change his posture and devotion toward the Lord. He would later be thrown into the lion's den, but God would deliver him unscathed. The king ordered his enemies and their families to be destroyed in the same lion's den they planned for Daniel's death. Additionally, because God had shown Himself so mightily on Daniel's behalf, the king decreed that everyone in his kingdom would fear Daniel's God.

Daniel's story proves that when our eyes are focused on God, our haters can't do anything with us. We may face persecution, betrayal, injustice, even the death of our dreams, loss of position, a negative change in plans, loss of health or loss of life, but neither of it will defeat us.

Every plot and scheme of the enemy against your life (even those from the enemies on your job) will not prosper. They are only setting you up for a come up. Stop fretting. Stop worrying. Your haters are elevation. After you endure the fire, promotion is coming.

Winning with Prayer
Dear Heavenly Father,

Thank You for being the Almighty God, full of miracles and wonder. You are The Lion of Judah. You are with me even in the lion's den, ensuring that no evil can harm me. Help me to praise You with reckless abandon. Help me to be unashamed in my worship. Scatter all of Your enemies in my life in Jesus' name. Amen.

Country
"Blessed is the nation whose God is the LORD [...]"
- Psalm 33:12

God First

Judges 6-8

And the LORD said unto him, Surely I will be with thee, and thou shalt smite the Midianites as one man.
- Judges 6:16

In some countries, it's not that God isn't worshipped. There are communities with churches on every corner and people who dedicate 15 minutes to talk to God every day. The acts of worship of God are there, but they are only acts. People still haven't abandoned their other gods. They have more allegiance to the god of money and god of success than to the Living God. They believe that their practice of spiritual disciplines makes up for their lack of total commitment, but God knows better. God asks Gideon, whose Hebrew name Jerrubaal actually includes the name "Baal" (a false god), to tear down his father's poles to that deity. The worship of Baal was so pervasive that the people even worshipped him alongside the one, true Living God. Because they didn't know God, they equated Him with Baal, a sin before the God who declared no god should be before Him. It was Israel's idolatry and disobedience to God that had invited Midianite persecution of their people. The Israelites were so oppressed by the Midianites that even their food had to be produced in secret for fear the Midianites would steal it. The great thing is that when the people cried out to God, He answered them and told them the reason for their oppression. He sent a prophet for them. He also sent Gideon, whom He would use to help deliver them.

As it was with the Israelites, so it is with us. Our nation's rebellion against God lies in the midst of our best attempts at piety. We sacrifice to the gods of sex, debauchery, and more, all before offering ritualistic services and traditions to the God we do not know. But God isn't mocked. Indeed, we are the only ones fooled. We've known for decades that our nations aren't under God but wonder where God is when our families, communities, schools, businesses, and governments face constant attacks. If we want to see God move for us, then we must take action in addition to prayer. We must be like Gideon and remove the physical idols and the spiritual idols from our hearts, even if it means we face opposition. There is hope for our nation, but it will be realized when we are serious about placing God back in first place in our hearts and our world.

Winning with Prayer
Dear Heavenly Father,

Thank You that even in the midst of despair there is hope. You cause barren lands to thrive again when we put You first. Help me to do my part. Help me to keep You at the helm of my world so we can experience Your goodness and grace. In Jesus' name. Amen.

Heal Our Land

Nehemiah 1

And they said unto me, The remnant that are left of the captivity there in the province are in great affliction and reproach: the wall of Jerusalem also is broken down, and the gates thereof are burned with fire. - Nehemiah 1:3

It's so easy to look at our native lands and lament the degradation of society. The hatred that manifests itself in the persistent racism, sexism, and phobias against mankind seems impenetrable. The breakdown of our families and communities as the glorification of lust and ungodly social roles are touted seem to place us daily on a collision course to meet an inevitable, destructive end. The constant diet of senseless violence, corruption, and misfortune can leave us wondering what, if anything, we can do to make a meaningful difference. Nehemiah, a Hebrew cupbearer for Babylonian King Artaxerxes, was confronted with the news that his beloved Jerusalem had been destroyed and knew that he had to do something. The remnant of his people had been taken in captivity, the protective walls had been broken down, and the gates to the city had been burned. Nehemiah immediately went before God with prayer and fasting and repented of sins committed by his people and himself. God would eventually grant him favor with the king and allow him and others to rebuild the physical walls of Jerusalem, They would also repair the spiritual breach between God and the people.

This is what must be done for our nation. God says in 2 Chronicles 7:14 that:

> "If My people, who are called by My name, shall humble themselves, and pray, and seek My face, and turn from their wicked ways; then will I hear from Heaven, and will forgive their sin, and will heal their land."

Our hopes for restoration of our broken land and its moral decadence rests in the ability of God's people to petition God to heal our land. It didn't matter that Nehemiah lived in royal comfort in a land far removed from the affliction of his homeland. His heart was still with his persecuted brothers and sisters in the place they had all called home. He was moved about their plight. Christians who live in relative comfort and those who take pride that they are separate from the world must recognize that God cares about people and the land. God has positioned us in places of comfort so that we can help those less fortunate. The great thing is that help is as simple as going before the Lord with a posture of humility and surrender to seek His face and make our petitions known.

Don't be discouraged about the decay of our nation and the world. Instead, commit to taking our issues to God in earnest prayer. We must take an honest assessment of our own sins and those of our country, and we must own them. We can no longer afford to downplay our sins individually or as a community, for these are the real culprits behind the degeneration we see. God has given His prescription for healing, and now we must act upon it. Our land will change for the better when God's people go on their knees and wait for His hand, not with more laws and rules. God wants to claim the land of our hearts. Let's exact meaningful change in the world as we partner with God to change nations with the power of righteous living and prayer.

Winning with Prayer
Dear Heavenly Father,

Thank You that You are El Shaddai, the Almighty God, and nothing is too hard for You. You see the problems of my world and have invited me to partner with You in its healing through my earnest prayers and righteous living. Help me to honestly assess my sins and those of my nation so that I can lead the charge of repentance. Thank You for Your promise of healing when I do. In Jesus' name, I pray. Amen.

Made in the USA
Columbia, SC
21 August 2023